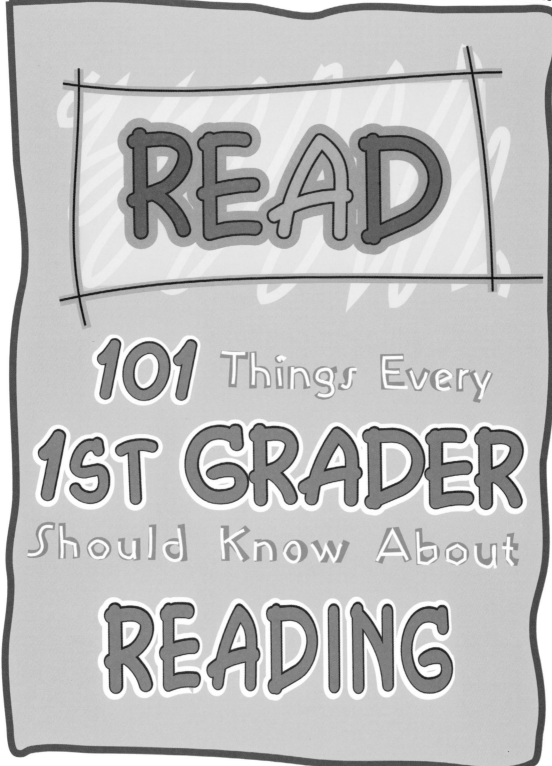

READ

101 Things Every 1ST GRADER Should Know About READING

Writers: Natalie Goldstein and Michele Warrence-Schreiber

Consultant: Elizabeth C. Stull, Ph.D.

active minds

Writer: Natalie Goldstein is a freelance writer and editor for children's educational books. She has contributed to dozens of activity books, textbooks, and other workbooks for many different publishers, including McGraw-Hill, Houghton Mifflin, Prentice Hall, and Scholastic. In addition, she holds a master's degree in education.

Writer: Michele Warrence-Schreiber holds a master's degree in the teaching of reading education. She is a freelance writer of educational material and teaches kindergarten and elementary school reading. She has contributed to a variety of publications and video projects, including those for Scholastic, Houghton Mifflin, UNICEF, and PBS teacher development videos.

Consultant: Elizabeth C. Stull holds a doctorate in early and middle childhood education specializing in curriculum. She has taught language, literacy, and children's literature at Ohio State University, and has written numerous activity books for teachers, including *Alligators to Zebras: Whole Language Activities for the Primary Grades, Kindergarten Teachers Survival Guide,* and *Multicultural Learning Activities: K–6.*

Illustrations by George Ulrich.

Louis Weber, CEO
Publications International, Ltd.
7373 North Cicero Avenue
Lincolnwood, Illinois 60712

www.myactiveminds.com

ISBN-13: 978-1-4127-9460-2
ISBN-10: 1-4127-9460-9

Manufactured in China.

8 7 6 5 4 3 2 1

Contents

Ready, Set, Read!

Dear Parents:

Starting 1st grade is an exciting time for children. They know the basics of reading, writing, and math and are ready for new challenges. They seem to want to know more about everything! Of course you want to give your child that special head start that is so important. This workbook will help your child

learn the basic skills of a vast array of reading concepts and processes—skills your child will build on in future learning.

Inside this workbook, children will find 101 fun-filled reading activities right at their fingertips. Each activity focuses on a different skill and provides your child with plenty of opportunity to practice that skill. The activities are arranged in order of difficulty, beginning with the most basic skills. This will help to build your child's confidence as he or she goes along. They'll feel a real sense of accomplishment as they complete each page.

Every activity is clearly labeled with the skill being taught. You will find skill keys written especially for you, the parent, at the bottom of each activity page. These skill keys give you information about what your child is learning.

Also, suggestions are provided for additional hands-on activities you may choose to do with your child. These offer fun, enjoyable opportunities to reinforce the skill being taught.

Children learn in a variety of ways. They are sure to appreciate the bright, exciting illustrations in this workbook. The pictures are not just fun—they also help visual learners develop their reading skills by giving them something to relate to. Children may also like to touch the pictures and say each word out loud. Such methods can be important aids in your child's learning process.

Your child can tackle some of the activities independently; in other cases you will need to read the directions for your child before he or she can complete the exercise. Each activity should be fun and enough of a challenge that it will be exciting for your child. Be patient and support your child in positive ways. Let them know it's all right to take a guess or pull back if they're unsure. And, of course, celebrate their successes with them. Learning should be an exciting and positive experience for everyone. Enjoy your time together as your child enhances his or her 1st-grade reading skills.

Abracadabra!

Connect the dots in ABC order to see what the magician has pulled from his hat. When you're finished, add color to your picture.

Skill:

Recognizing letters in alphabetical order

Answers on page 121.

Buddy Up!

The lowercase letters have been separated from their uppercase partners.

Use a different color to color each pair of letter partners. When you're done, you'll have 13 pairs of letters.

Skill:

Matching uppercase letters with lowercase letters: A–M

Answers on page 121.

Alphabet Soup!

These letters are all mixed up! Find a lowercase buddy for each uppercase letter. Write the letter pairs on the lines below. Then cross them out in the soup. The first one is done for you.

Nn

Skill:

Matching uppercase letters with lowercase letters: N–Z

Answers on page 121.

Lost and Found

Don't lose your suitcase!
Fill in your bag tag.

Write your first and last
name on the first line,
your address on the
second line, and your
phone number on the
third line.

Skills:

Writing first and last
name, address, and
phone number

Name

First   Last

Shola   *Odolomenun*

Address

40 Salem Street

Phone Number

3390276177

Answers will vary.

Alphabet Monkey in the Middle

Do you know your ABCs?

Write the letters that come before and after the ones written below.

Skill:

Sequencing letters in alphabetical order

a b c   g h i   s t u   k l m

Answers on page 121.

Who Comes First?

Help the teacher figure out who comes first. Put the children in alphabetical order. Write their names in the correct order on the lines below.

_____   _____   _____

_____   _____

Skill:

Sequencing words in alphabetical order

Answers on page 121.

X Marks the Spot

This letter's name is **X.** But if it is at the end of a word, the **x** says **ks.** Color the pictures whose name ends in the **ks** sound. Connect all the colored pictures to lead Rex to his tux.

Answers on page 121.

Can You Hear?

Everyone is talking! Circle the beginning sound in each word.

Skill:

Understanding sound/symbol correspondence

Answers on page 121.

Name That Sound!

Look at the pictures.

What beginning sound do you hear?

Circle the letter that makes that sound.

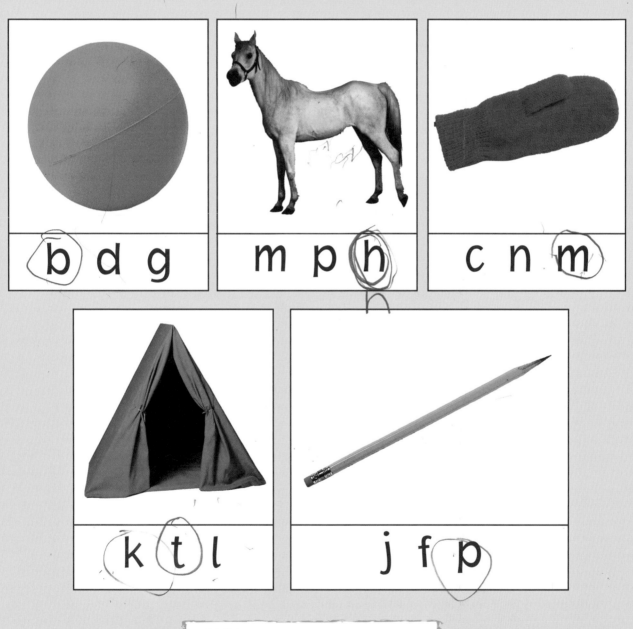

b d g

m p h

c n m

k t l

j f p

Skill:

Identifying initial consonant sounds

Answers on page 121.

Same or Different?

Say the words out loud. Two of the words in each group start with the same sound. One does not. Circle the word that begins with a different sound.

boy	paper	dog
baby	chair	toy
doll	pen	toe
man	sink	
milk	seed	
car	bed	

Skill:

Discriminating between initial consonant sounds

Answers on page 121.

Listen to the End!

Can you hear it?

Two of the words in each group end with the same sound.

One word ends with a different sound.

Write the word with a different ending on the line below each group of words. Read those words to get the message!

(Hint: Use an uppercase letter for the first word.)

put
dad
red

_____

ten
your
men

_____

toys
cup
lip

_____

me
see
away

_____

Skill:

Discriminating between ending sounds

Answers on page 122.

Teacher's Pet

Help the teacher get organized. Look at the pictures. Say the words. Draw a line from each toy to the toy box with the correct beginning sound.

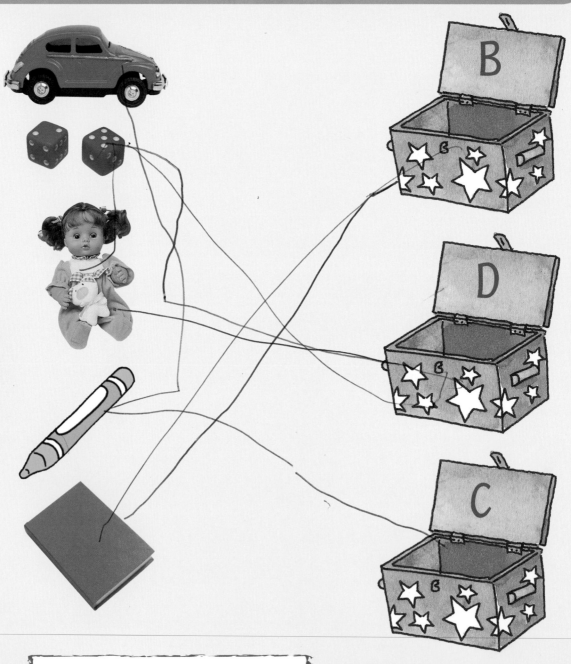

Skill:

Identifying sound/symbol relationships

Answers on page 122.

Sad Dad

Dad can't find his keys! Help him find the right keys. Color in the keys that end in **-ad.**

Skill:

Identifying words in the **-ad** family

Answers on page 122.

Stay and Play!

Words that end in **-ay** are in the same family. Help the children finish their game of hopscotch by coloring the squares with **-ay** words on them.

hay

baby

jay

day

clay

may

fly

Skill:

Identifying words in the **-ay** family

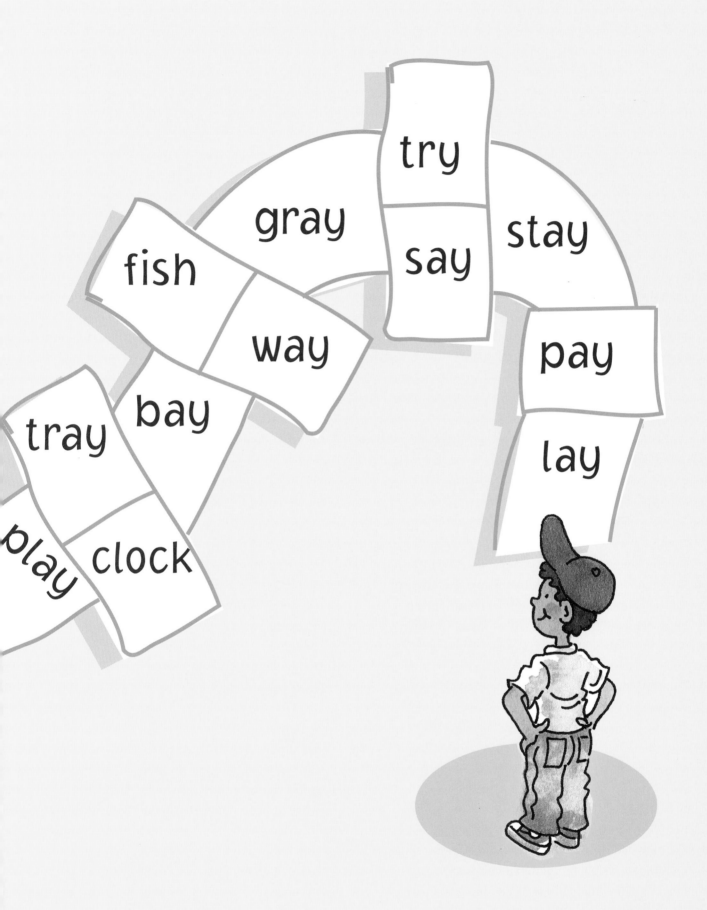

Oh Well

Find the words that end in **–ell,** and put a circle around them.

The shell they were trying to sell fell into the well! Ring the bell! Who can we tell?

Skill:

Identifying words in the **–ell** family

Answers on page 122.

Spin It!

Start at the top of the wheel and go around. How many words can you find that end in **-ot?** Write them on the lines below.

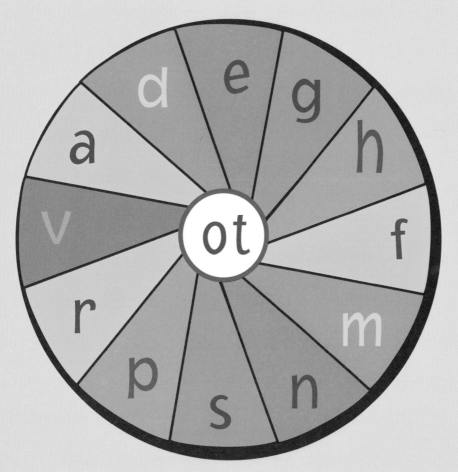

Skill:

Identifying words in the **-ot** family

Answers on page 122.

Buried Treasure

Help the sailor find the buried treasure! Read all the words. Then draw a line from the sailor to the buried treasure by going through all the words that end with **-ill.**

have

this

bill

fill

hill

Skill:

Identifying words in the **-ill** family

was

play

they

with

will

still

pill

Answers on page 122.

Pumpkin Patch

Read the word in each pumpkin. If the word ends with **-ake**, color the pumpkin orange. Color the other pumpkins green.

cake

there

said

what

take

can

each

bake

your

make

awake

fake

Skill:

Identifying words in the **-ake** family

26

Answers on page 122.

Be a Word Wizard!

Make new words by changing the beginning sounds of the words below. Use the picture clues to help you. Write the new word on the line. The first one is done for you.

fake

cake

shell

bake

bill

hot

bay

Skill:

Changing the beginning letters of word families to make new words

Answers on page 122.

Color It In!

The letter **c** has two different sounds. Listen for the hard **c** sound in **cat.** Listen for the soft **c** sound in **pencil.**

Color the hard **c** words blue. Color the soft **c** words orange.

What do you see?

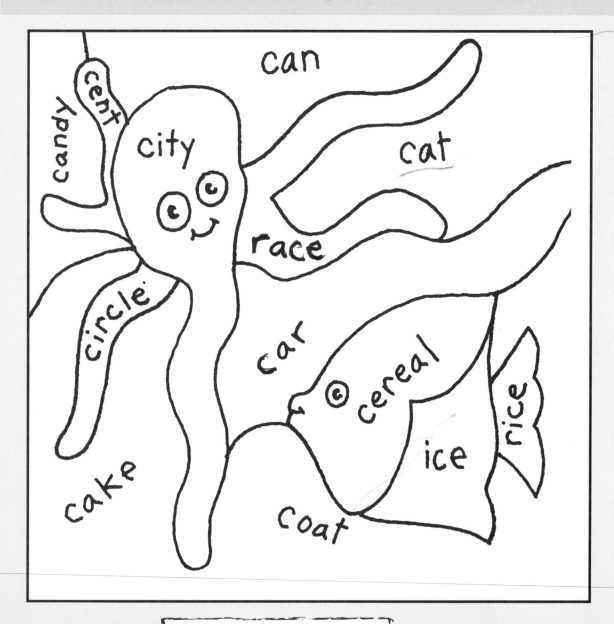

can
candy
cent
city
cat
race
circle
car
cereal
rice
ice
cake
coat

Skill:

Recognizing that the letter **c** has a hard sound and a soft sound

Answers on page 122.

Gone Fishing!

The letter **g** has two different sounds.
Listen for the hard **g** sound in **Gabe.**
Listen for the soft **g** sound in **Ginger.**

Help Gabe catch all the fish that have the hard **g** sound.
Help Ginger catch all the fish that have the soft **g** sound.
Color Gabe's fish blue. Color Ginger's fish red.

 game

 go

 gerbil

 girl

 gate

 germ

 goose

 giant

 giraffe

 dragon

 gem

 page

Skill:

Recognizing that the letter **g** has a hard sound and a soft sound

Answers on page 122.

Name Game

Write your name in a line from top to bottom. Now use the letters in your name to make up words that describe you. If your name is **Sam,** you would think of words that begin with **S, A,** and **M.**

Soccer player
Awesome
Messy!

Lovely
Intelligent
Likable
Athletic

Lucky
Unusual
Kind
Energetic

Interesting
Active
Nice

Parents:

Do this one with your child. For an added challenge, try this activity with your last name.

Skill:

Using letters as initial sounds in words

30

Answers will vary.

Over the River!

Some vowels make short sounds. Listen for the short vowels in **cat, pet, pin, mop,** and **cup.**

Help the scout leader cross the river. Color the stones with short vowels gray. Color the rest of the stones blue. If you color the stones correctly, the scout leader will have a path across the river.

Skill:

Identifying short vowel sounds

Answers on page 122.

Looking for Long Vowels

Some vowels make long sounds. Listen for the long vowel sounds in **rake, seal, pine, rope,** and **tube.**

Say the name of each picture. Circle the pictures whose names have a long vowel sound.

Skill:

Identifying long vowel sounds

32

Answers on page 123.

Vowel Match

Draw a line from the picture to its beginning sound.

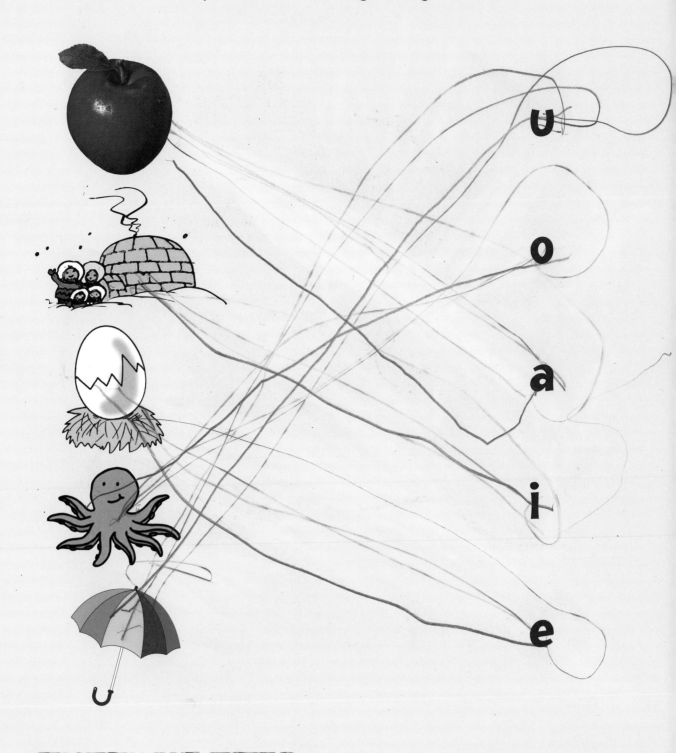

Skill:

Matching words to beginning vowels

Answers on page 123.

You Can Do It!

Look at the pictures.

Write in the missing vowel to make words.

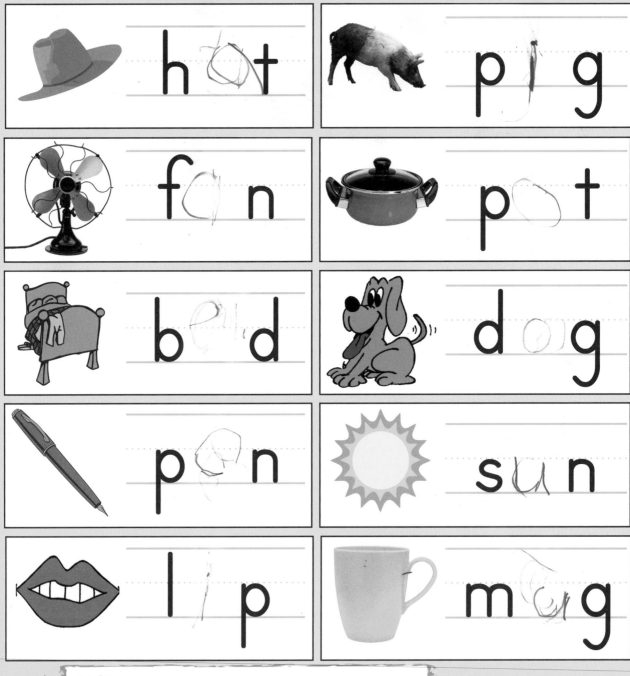

h a t

p i g

f a n

p o t

b e d

d o g

p e n

s u n

l i p

m u g

Skill:

Recognizing that medial (middle) vowels are needed to make three-letter consonant-vowel-consonant words

Answers on page 123.

Vowel in the Middle!

The vowels are stuck in the bog! Change the middle letter to make new words. The first one is done for you.

I go to the **bog** .

I go to the b   g with my b   g .

I go to the b   g with my b   g

to get a b   g .

I go to the b   g with my b   g

to get a b   g that is b   g .

Skill:

Changing the medial (middle) vowel creates new words

Answers on page 123.

Who's in Control?

Some vowels are controlled by the letter **r.** That means their sound is different because you can hear the **r** when you read the word.

Help Mary get control of her dog. Color the stones that have r-controlled vowels. The first one is done for you.

sir

bird

mother

bark

her

cat

play

skip

they

star

park

burn

born

dark

don't

the

fur

car

far

jar

Answers on page 123.

Let's Take a Walk!

Say the word **coal.** Do you hear the long **o** sound? Usually, when two vowels are side by side you hear the sound the first one makes. Remember it this way: When two vowels go walking, the first one does the talking.

Say the name of each picture. Color the pictures where you hear the name of the first vowel.

Skill:

Sounding out vowel pairs

Answers on page 123.

Make Magic!

Listen to the vowel sound in the word **kit.** Add an **e,** and say the word **kite.** The vowel sound changed. The **e** at the end of **kite** makes the vowel say its name!

Say the name of each picture below. Then write a new word on the line by adding the magic **e.** Read the new words. Do you hear the long vowel sounds?

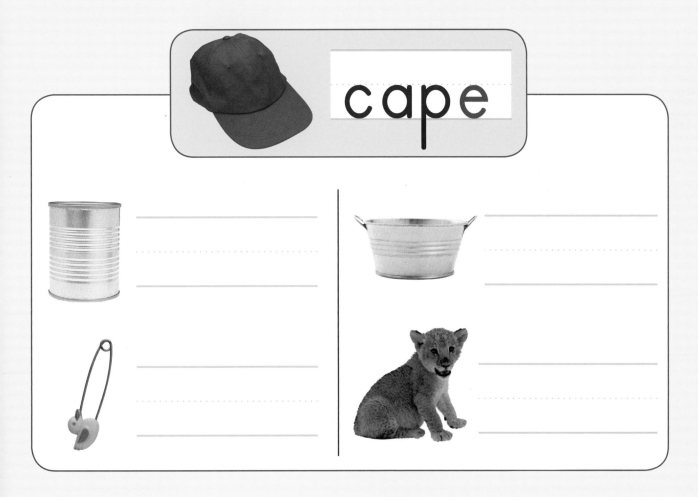

cape

Answers on page 123.

Calling All Vowels!

Solve the riddles!

Fill in the blanks with an **a, e, i, o,** or **u.**

Why did the girl give the boy a dog biscuit?

Because he was the teacher's p___t.

What insect does well in school?

The spelling b_____ .

What can you catch that doesn't run?

A c___ld.

Why did the class clown eat the dollar his mother gave him to take to school?

It was his l___nch money!

Skill:

Recognizing that vowels are needed to make words

Answers on page 123.

Oooo La La!

Listen for the **oo** sound in **broom.** Now listen for the **oo** sound in **good.** Do you hear the difference?

Read each word. Color the flowers that rhyme with **broom** red. Color the flowers that rhyme with **good** orange.

foot

raccoon

moon

wood

spoon

book

boot

Skill:

Discriminating between the different sounds of **oo**

Answers on page 123.

Check the Ads

Help make a shopping list!

Look at the newspaper, and find six things you can buy that begin with the letter **P.** Write them on the lines below.

....

....

....

....

....

....

Answers on page 123.

Guess It!

Finish the **sh-** and **ch-** words below.
Use the hints and pictures to help you.

It is a sh_____.
Hint: You wear it.

It is a sh_____.
Hint: It's like a boat.

It is a sh_____.
Hint: You find it on the beach.

It is a ch_____.
Hint: It's below your mouth.

It is a ch_____.
Hint: You sit on it.

It is ch_____.
Hint: You can write with it on a board.

Skill:

Identifying **sh-** and **ch-** blends

Answers on page 123.

Listen Carefully!

How does it begin? Draw a line from the picture to its matching letters.

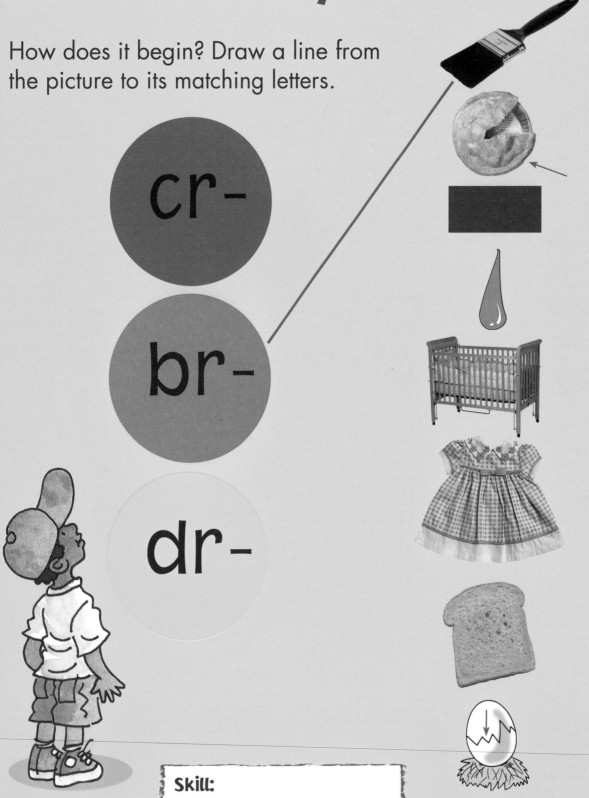

cr-

br-

dr-

Answers on page 124.

Greasy Fries

Read the crazy sentence below. Underline all the words that begin with the **gr-** blend. Then put a ☐ around the words that begin with the **fr-** blend.

Grandpa Frank and Grandma Fran are grumpy grandparents when they fry french fries and grease gets on the ground!

Skill:

Identifying **gr-** and **fr-** blends

Answers on page 124.

Twins

Troy and Priscilla are twins.
They share everything—except their birthday presents!

Draw a line from the toys that begin with the **tr-** blend to Troy. Draw a line from the toys that begin with the **pr-** blend to Priscilla.

Troy

Priscilla

TRUCK

PRINCE

PRINCESS

PRETZEL

TRAIN

TREE

Skill:

Identifying **tr-** and **pr-** blends

Answers on page 124.

Night Sky

Color the words that begin with **gl-** blue.
Color the words that begin with **sl-** yellow.
Color the words that begin with **pl-** green.
What do you see?

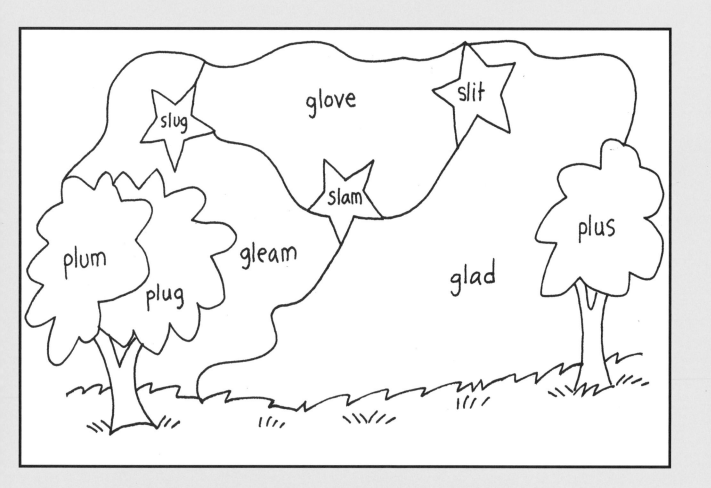

Skill:

Identifying **gl-**, **pl-**, and **sl-** blends

Answers on page 124.

Balloon Blends

black

blond

club

clown

blue

Skill:

Identifying **bl-**, **cl-**, and **fl-** blends

Help the girls get their balloons back! Color ballons with the **fl-** blend yellow, the **bl-** blend blue, and the **cl-** blend purple. Then write the words from the balloons on the lines.

Answers on page 124.

Let It Snow

Are you ready to go out in the snow?
Use one of the words from the list to
finish each sentence.

slope
snowboard
sticks
skates
smile
skiis

Will you go to the ice rink or down the big hill?

Do you want two _____ for the rink?

Do you want two _____ for the hill?

Do you want poles?

Sometimes we call them _____.

Only one?

When you use this board in the snow, it

is called a _____.

Are you ready?

Put a _____ on your face!

Are you heading for the big hill?

Sometimes we call this a _____.

Skill:

Identifying **s-** blends

Answers on page 124.

I Scream, You Scream!

Finish this story using the words below. You will use one word more than once.

It was hot. All I wanted was a treat.

I ran home. I heard someone _____ !

The door was locked.

I broke the _____ door to get in.

I got a _____ on my arm.

Then I saw why my sister yelled.

Her banana _____ was on the floor!

It had gone _____ !

She said, "I _____ , you _____ ,

we all _____ for ice cream!"

split   scream

scratch   screen

splat

Skill:

Identifying **spl-** and **scr-** blends

Answers on page 124.

Guess and Check

Write a word from the box to solve each riddle. Use the pictures to help you.

A kite flies on the end of it.

What is it? A _____.

You can drink through this.

What is it? A _____.

spring

sprint

strike

string

straw

You do it when you run fast.

What do you do? You _____.

It is the season that comes after winter.

What is it? It is _____.

If you swing the bat but miss the ball, it is a _____.

Skill:

Identifying **str-** and **spr-** blends

Answers on page 124.

Word Sort

Read the words in the box below. Use the first vowel in each word to decide where to write the word. Cross out the words as you use them.

is	in	you	that	it	up
he	was	for	on	are	us
~~as~~	with	his	they	I	
at	be	this	have	from	
of	and	a	to	the	

a	e	i	o	u
as				

Answers on page 124.

Word Play

Find and circle the words in the box below. Remember: The words can either be across or down.

or	by	but	what	were	when
one	word	not	use	there	yours
had					

```
W H E N T G B R P E L L O U S E
P T C A E F U L W H A T N L Y S
Q S G O N O T E A B Y E E G O V
T H E R E W O R D A L E S W U T
H A D F U N K E Y W E R E F R S
M O N K E Y S P F E L L A K S S
```

Unscramble the letters below to make words.

nac _____   na _____   od _____

dsai _____   chea _____   ohw _____

ew _____   chiwh _____   hteir _____

lal _____   hse _____   fi _____

Skill:

Identifying sight words: group 2

Answers on page 124.

Order, Order

Sort these words! Write each word from the box next to the correct letter below. The first one is done for you.

him	them	write	two
will	some	her	~~go~~
into	make	other	out
these	like	more	would
then	time	to	

g　go

i

m

s

t

t

w

h

l

o

t

t

w

w

h

m

o

t

t

Skills:

Identifying/alphabetizing sight words: group 3

Answers on page 124.

Word Detective

Read the words below. Find and circle them in the puzzle. Remember: The words can either be across or down.

number	first	how	come
no	water	find	made
way	been	long	may
could	all	down	part
people	who	day	
my	oil	did	
than	its	get	

N U M B E R A B N O C D W A Y E

F C O U L D G H P E O P L E I J

M Y K L T H A N M N F I R S T O

P W A T E R Q R B E E N T S A L

A D V W H O X W O I L A Z I T S

R O H O W C D F I N D L F D A Y

T W D I D I J G E T K L C O M E

M N M A D E O P M A Y Q R P A R

T G H N P T A L O N G H C J L M

Answers on page 124.

Label It

Look at the pictures. Write the beginning letter on each label.

Answers on page 124.

Find It!

Read the clues to help the class solve the problems! First, find the picture that solves the clue. Then circle the letter and write it in the alphabet chart.

Skills:

Recognizing letter/sound relationships and beginning sounds for: **b, g, k, m, n, v, x**

a _ c d e f _ h i
j _ l _ _ o p q r
s t u _ w _ y z

Clues

I'm thinking of something that begins with a **b.** We read them!

I'm thinking of something that begins with a **g.** It's an animal that we have in the classroom!

I'm thinking of something that begins with a **k.** You fly it outside!

I'm thinking of something that begins with an **m.** You wear them to keep your hands warm!

I'm thinking of something that begins with an **n.** You find it on a face!

I'm thinking of something that begins with a **v.** You give it to your friend on a special day!

I'm thinking of something that begins with an **x.** It's a picture of bones!

Be My Valentine

Answers on page 124.

Mixed Up

Everything is mismatched! The labels on the pictures are all wrong. Cross out the letters and write the ones you hear at the beginning of each word.

Skills:

Recognizing letter/sound relationships and beginning sounds for **b, d, p, s, y**

Answers on page 125.

What Is Your Name?

My name is Li - la! Clap out how many word parts you hear.

Li – la has two word parts or **syllables** in her name.

Clap out the names below, and write the number of syllables you hear in each name.

Ellie, Anna, Sofia, Kelsey, Madison, John Rafael

What is your name?

How many syllables do you hear in your name?

Ellie

Anna

Sofia

Kelsey

Madison

John Rafael

Skill:

Working with syllables

Answers on page 125.

Keep On Track!

Help the conductor put the train cars back together again. Read each syllable. Put them together to make words. Then write the new word.

> **Skill:**
>
> Using syllables to put words back together visually

Answers on page 125.

What Is It?

A noun is a naming word. Nouns name a person, place, or thing. Some nouns stand for a single thing. These are **singular** nouns.

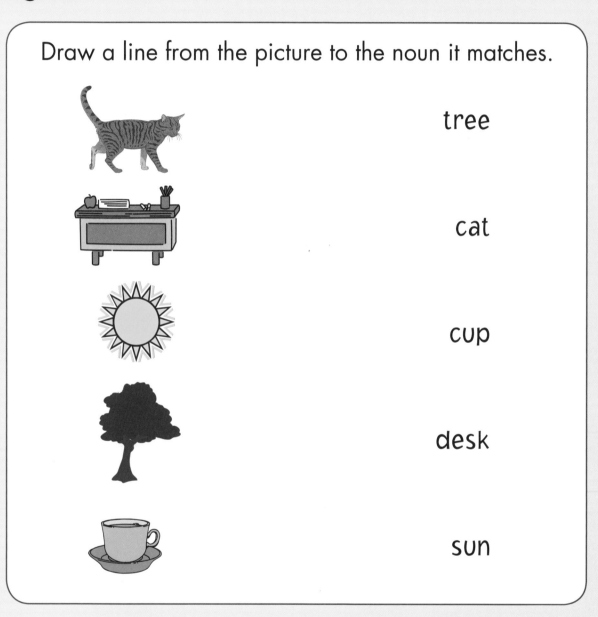

Draw a line from the picture to the noun it matches.

tree

cat

cup

desk

sun

Skill:

Identifying parts of speech: nouns for things

Answers on page 125.

A Day Trip

Some nouns are the names of places. **School, home,** and **park** are nouns for places.

The people in the car are on a day trip. Where do they go? Use the words in the box to find out. Write one word from the box next to each picture.

lake	store	home	park

We left _____.

We went to the

_____.

We went to the

_____ .

We went to the

_____ .

Then we came back

_____ .

We had fun!

Answers on page 125.

What's My Name?

Streets have names. Towns have names. People have names. Pets have names. What is your name? The name of a person or place is a kind of noun. It is called a **proper noun.**

A proper noun always begins with a capital letter.

Emma

Bill

Rex

Wall Street

Circle the picture that goes with the proper noun.

Pam Smith

Main Street

Mr. Brown

Bob

my pet Fluffy

Elton School

Skill:

Identifying parts of speech: proper nouns

Answers on page 125.

Two Together

Some big words are made of two small words.
The new word is called a **compound word.**

bird + cage = birdcage

Look at each pair of words below. Join the two small words to make one compound word. Write the new word.

base + ball = _____

rain + coat = _____

cup + cake = _____

mail + box = _____

flower + pot = _____

Skill:

Making compound words

Answers on page 125.

More Than One

Some nouns stand for more than one thing. These are **plural** nouns. How do you write plural nouns? You add an **s** to the end of a noun. Many nouns get an **s** at the end to show more than one.

one cat   two cats

Circle the plural noun that goes with the picture.

pet   dog   dogs

socks   foot   sock

apple   apples   red

pigs   pig   piggy

Skill:

Making nouns plural by adding **s**

Answers on page 125.

More Than One–Again

Some plural nouns get **es** at the end to show more than one.

Nouns that end in **s, sh, ch, x,** or **z** get **es** at the end to show more than one.

dish   dishes

fox   fox**es**

Add **s** or **es** to the noun to show more than one.

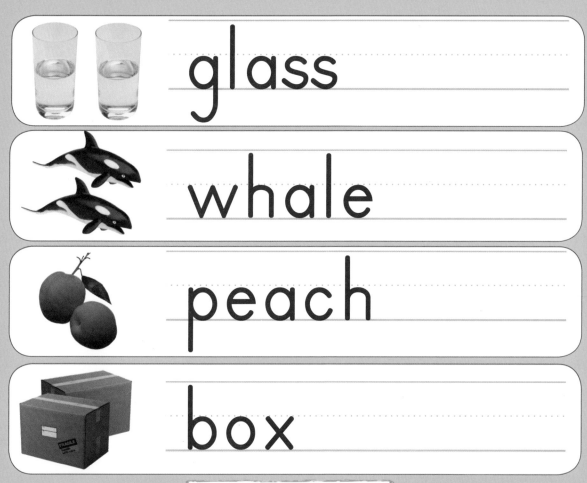

glass

whale

peach

box

Skill:

Making nouns plural with **es**

Answers on page 125.

I Can Do It!

Some words are action words. They tell what people and things do. Action words are called **verbs.**

Some verbs are

dance | walk

Write the verb that goes with the picture.

I can _____.

run   girl   fast

I can _____.

boy   sing   hair

I can _____.

write   pen   book

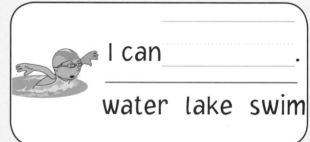

I can _____.

water   lake   swim

Skill:

Identifying verbs: present tense regular

Answers on page 125.

I Can Do It Again!

Underline the verb in each sentence.

The baby sleeps.

The boy reads the book.

He plays basketball.

The bird sings in a tree.

We bake cookies.

Skill:

Identifying verbs: present tense regular

Answers on page 125.

What Did You Do?

Some verbs tell what you did in the past. They are called **past-tense** verbs.

Most past-tense verbs end with **d** or **ed.**

Write the past-tense verb that goes in the sentence.

The boy _Played_ basketball.

(played) jump play

The boy _dreamed_ of candy.

sleep (dreamed) dream

The baby _rolled_ the ball.

roll (rolled) round

The girl _painted_ a picture.

(painted) paint brush

Skill:

Identifying verbs: past tense regular

Answers on page 125.

What Else Did You Do?

Some past-tense verbs do not end with **d** or **ed.**

Read the word pairs in the box. Each pair of verbs shows the present tense and the past tense. Say each word pair aloud.

Present Tense	Past Tense
go	went
eat	ate
give	gave
tell	told
run	ran

Write the past-tense verb that goes with each sentence.

Jim **went** to the beach.

(went)   go

Billy **ate** an apple.

eat   (ate)

Jill **gave** her friend a present.

give   (gave)

Skill:

Identifying verbs: past tense irregular

To Be or Not To Be

The verb **to be** is special. You use this verb every day. The verb **to be** is different from other verbs.

Read each sentence below. The **to be** verb is underlined in each sentence.

Present tense of to be	Past tense of to be
I <u>am</u> happy.	I <u>was</u> happy.
He <u>is</u> happy.	He <u>was</u> happy.
Pam <u>is</u> happy.	Pam <u>was</u> happy.
It <u>is</u> sunny.	It <u>was</u> sunny.
You <u>are</u> nice.	You <u>were</u> nice.
We <u>are</u> friends.	We <u>were</u> friends.
They <u>are</u> happy.	They <u>were</u> happy.

Present Tense of To Be

Write the word that fits the sentence.

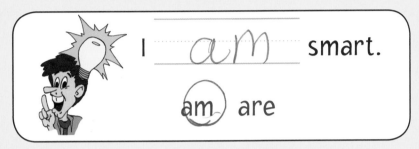

I _am_ smart.

(am) are

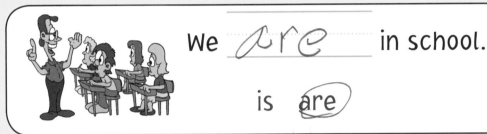

We _are_ in school.

is (are)

Past Tense of To Be

Circle the word that fits the sentence.

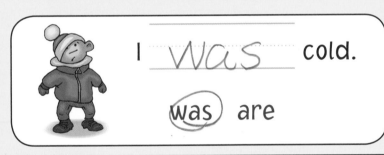

I _was_ cold.

(was) are

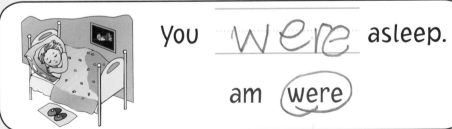

You _were_ asleep.

am (were)

Skill:

Using the verb **to be:** present and past tense.

Answers on page 126.

Pronoun Practice

You know about nouns. Nouns are naming words. A **pronoun** is a word that stands for a noun. A pronoun may replace a noun. Read the sentences. The noun and the pronoun that replaces it are underlined.

The cup is full.	It is full.
The girl is happy.	She is happy.
The boy has fun.	He has fun.
Emma is my friend.	You are my friend.
Bob and I like pizza.	We like pizza.
Liz and Pam play.	They play.

Draw a line from the picture to the pronoun that matches it.

it   she   he   they

Skill:

Matching nouns and pronouns

Answers on page 126.

Let's Agree

A noun or pronoun must match a verb. The verb must agree with the noun or pronoun. Nouns for one thing match verbs that end in **s.** The pronouns **he, she,** and **it** also match verbs that end in **s.** The following sentences show how verbs match different nouns and pronouns.

I talk.	You talk.
She talks. Jane talks.	We talk.
He talks. Bob talks.	They talk.
It talks.	The toy talks.

Write the word that fits the sentence.

I _____ to school every day.

walk   walks

The kids _____ ball.

plays   play

She _____ rope.

jumps   jump

Skill:

Understanding subject-verb agreement: present tense

Answers on page 126.

No, No, No

Some words mean no. These words are called **negative** words. You use negative words every day.

> Read the sentences. The negative words are underlined.
>
> I have <u>no</u> candy. | I do <u>not</u> want lunch.

Write the word that fits the sentence.

I have _____ money.

no   not

Lily does _____ watch TV after school.

not   no

I _____ want to go to sleep!

no   never

I do _____ want to ride my bike now.

never   not

Skill:

Using negatives

Answers on page 126.

Shorties

Sometimes two small words go together. Then a vowel is left out of one word. The little ' mark takes the place of the missing vowel. These kinds of words are called **contractions.**

You use contractions every day.	
I am happy.	I'm happy.
It is a good story.	It's a good story.

Fill in the blank. Write a contraction using the two words under the sentence.

An elephant _____ small.

is   not

_____ not hungry.

I   am

I _____ want to go out today.

do   not

_____ raining cats and dogs.

It   is

Skill:

Contractions

Color Me!

Some words are the names of colors. Circle the color words in these sentences. Use the sentences to help you color the picture.

The grass and the leaves on the tree are green.

The tree trunk is brown.

The ducks are yellow.

The sky and pond are blue.

The flowers are red.

Answers on page 126.

Clowning Around

Some words describe nouns or pronouns. These words are called **adjectives.** Read the sentences. The adjectives are underlined.

I like my <u>red</u> shoes.   I have a <u>small</u> puppy.

Jill is a <u>smart</u> girl.   We painted the <u>old</u> house.

What is this clown like? Color the balloons with adjectives to find out!

balloons: old, toy, silly, funny, man, loud, balloon, circus, shoe, tree, happy, baby

Answers on page 126.

Small Poems

Some words sound the same. Read the pairs of words. Say the words out loud. These words rhyme.

pair—chair   say—day   meat—eat

A poem has words that rhyme. Read each poem. Circle the word that rhymes.

Every day we like to ___.	play try
My mother bakes the very best ___.	cooks cakes
At the end of the sheet I see my ___.	feet trees
When I see the sun shine it makes me feel ___.	fun fine
I am so bright I can read and ___.	write rate

Skill:

Recognizing rhyming words

Answers on page 126.

Riddles

Look at the pictures and words in the box. Each word answers a riddle. Write the word that answers each riddle.

snail   nose   kite   bed   mouse

You lie in me.
You rest your head.
You dream in me.
I am your _____.

When I move
I leave a trail.
I live in a shell.
I am a _____.

I am small and gray
And may live in a house.
I love to eat cheese.
I am a _____.

It sits on your face
And sometimes it blows.
It helps you smell things.
It is your _____.

Skill:

Recognizing rhymes through riddles

I go high in the sky
Because I'm so light.
I fly on a string.
I am a _____.

Sounds the Same

Some words sound the same. But they have different meanings. They may be spelled differently. Read the two words. Say each word. Do they sound the same? What does each word mean?

 son

 sun

ant—a bug aunt—a relative	flower—a bloom flour—something you bake with
no—a negative know—to understand	pair—two of something pear—a fruit

Circle the word whose meaning fits the sentence.

 I have a ___ of socks.
pair   pear

 It is a pretty ___.
flower   flour

 The ___ ran across the floor.
aunt   ant

 Liz is eating a ___.
pair   pear

 I ___ how to read.
no   know

 I ___ a bird from my window.
see   sea

Skill:

Understanding homophones

Answers on page 126.

Look-Alikes

Some words look the same, but they have different meanings. They may sound different too.

The word **bark** sounds the same. It has the same letters. But it has different meanings. What does each bark mean?

the bark of a tree   the bark of a dog

Read each sentence. Circle the picture that best completes the sentence.

The boy threw the ___.

ball   ball

I can hear the school bell ___.

ring   ring

A ___ flies at night.

bat   bat

I write with a ___.

pen   pen

Skill:

Understanding homographs

Answers on page 126.

Some words have the same meaning. For example, **tired** and **sleepy** mean the same thing. Help the movers get from the truck to the house by putting a line through each box with words that mean the same thing.

Skill:

Identifying synonyms

Different Meanings

Some words have opposite meanings. For example, the words **up** and **down** are opposites. They have opposite meanings.

Look at the pictures. Draw a line to the word that means the opposite.

light

dark

short

sad

happy

tall

cold

hot

small

fast

slow

big

Skill:

Identifying antonyms

Answers on page 126.

What Happens First?

Some things happen in order. One thing happens first. Something happens second. Another thing happens last. Look at the pictures in each row. Write numbers in the boxes to show the correct order of events.

Skill:

Sequencing

Answers on page 126.

Then What Happens?

A story has a beginning, a middle, and an end. A story is told in order. The order tells what happens at the beginning, what happens in the middle, and what happens at the end.

Look at the pictures. Read the sentences. They are in order.

Beginning

Bill is tired.

Middle

Bill gets ready for bed.

End

Bill goes to sleep.

Look at the pictures. They tell a story. But the story is not in order. Draw a line from the picture to the word that tells the order.

Middle   **End**   **Beginning**

Skill:

Understanding parts of a story

Answers on page 127.

Story Words

Some words tell you the order of a story. Some of these words are

first   before   then   after

Look at the pictures. Read the sentences. Draw a line under the word that tells the order of the story.

First, Ann gets up in the morning.

Before Ann goes to school, she eats breakfast.

Then Ann is in school all day.

After school, Ann does her homework.

Skill:

Recognizing sequence/order words

Answers on page 127.

What Is a Sentence?

A sentence tells a complete thought. A sentence has a noun or a pronoun. A noun or pronoun is called the **subject** of a sentence. A sentence has a verb. The verb tells what the subject does.

I like

Fast ride

We hang on tight.

We like

Read the words. Color each car that has a complete sentence.

The ride goes fast.

Roller coasters are fun.

Skill:

Identifying complete sentences: subject-verb

92

Answers on page 127.

What Else Is in a Sentence?

A sentence must have a subject and a verb. Sometimes a sentence must have other words. The other words tell about the sentence. The other words are important to the meaning of the sentence.

The cow jumped over the moon.	The cow jumped over the
You need this word. ───────↑ It tells what the cow did. This is a complete sentence.	What did the cow jump over? This sentence does not tell you. This is not a complete sentence.

Draw a line under each complete sentence.

 The hen lays an egg. | The hen lays an

 The boy lunch | The boy eats lunch.

 We run to the top of

We run to the top of the hill.

 The girl wants some of the

The girl wants some of the crayons.

Skill:

Identifying complete sentences: predicate

Answers on page 127.

93

Put On a Cap

The first word in a sentence always begins with a capital letter.

 **K**ittens like to play. |  **M**y house is yellow.

Look at the picture. Read the sentence. Fill in the circle next to the word that should begin with a capital letter.

the monkey hangs in the tree.
The ◯ Monkey ◯ Tree ◯

my mother is a doctor.
Mother ◯ My ◯ Doctor ◯

dad got a new car.
new ◯ Car ◯ Dad ◯

this is my picture.
My ◯ This ◯ Picture ◯

Skill:

Beginning a sentence with a capital letter

94

Answers on page 127.

End With a Dot

Some sentences end with a dot. The dot is called a **period.**

> Mike went to the store.
> He got some milk.

Read the two sentences. One sentence is a complete sentence. Mark a period at the end of the complete sentence.

Meg has new shoes ☐

Meg has new ☐

_____

Bears love to eat honey ☐

Bears love to honey ☐

_____

Mark hit the ☐

Mark hit the ball ☐

Deb rows her boat ☐

Deb her boat ☐

_____

Ants are very strong ☐

Ants are very ☐

_____

It time ☐

It is time for lunch ☐

Skill:

Using punctuation: period

Write a Sentence

A sentence tells a complete thought. A sentence has a subject and verb. A sentence may have other important words. The first word in a sentence begins with a capital letter. There is a period at the end of a sentence.

the	a	jump	ball	throws	boy	girl
ice cream	likes	eats	dog	picks	in	play
an	garden	catches	to	cone	rope	flower

Look at the pictures. Write a sentence about each picture. You can use the words in the box to help you write the sentences, or you may use your own words.

Skill:

Writing a simple sentence

Answers will vary.

What Is the Question?

A question is a sentence that asks something. Most questions use question words.

who   what   where   why   when   how

A question ends with a question mark. Trace the question mark. Then write a question mark.

? ?

Read each sentence. Put a question mark after sentences that ask something. Put a period after sentences that tell something.

 Who is there

 What do you want to eat

 We ate pizza for lunch

 I'm looking for my baseball

Skills:

Identifying questions and using correct punctuation

Answers on page 127.

One After Another

Some words are connecting words. They connect two things in a sentence. These words are called **conjunctions.**

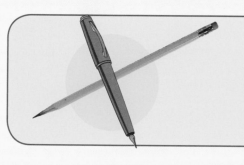

And is a connecting word.

I have a pen. I have a pencil.
I have a pen **and** pencil.

Read the two sentences. Use **and** to write them as one sentence.

I like soccer. I like baseball.

I like ....

The kitten is cute. The kitten is furry.

The kitten is ....

The popcorn is hot. The popcorn is salty.

The popcorn is ....

At the zoo I saw zebras. At the zoo I saw lions.

At the zoo I saw ....

Skill:

Using the conjunction **and**

Answers on page 127.

What's the Main Idea?

A story is about something. The main idea tells what a story is all about. Read the paragraph. The main idea is underlined.

main idea

Meg and her dog love to play together. They roll around on the grass. They play catch. They even race. Meg's dog always wins!

- -

Read each story. Circle the sentence that tells the main idea.

Joe is so busy. He goes to school all day. Then he plays football with the school team. When he gets home, it is time to eat dinner. Then he must do his homework. Before he knows it, it is time for bed.

Joe likes football.   Joe is very busy.   Joe goes to school.

Alice got her favorite seat on the school bus today. Then the cafeteria was serving apple pie for dessert. Alice loves apple pie. After school, her mom took her out for ice cream. It was a great day!

Alice takes the bus to school.   Alice's mom likes ice cream.
Alice had a great day.

Skill:

Identifying the main idea of a paragraph

Answers on page 127.

People in a Story

Many stories are about people. The people in a story are called **characters.** What a character does tells you what kind of person the character is. Read the short story. Then answer the questions.

 Tom walks home from school. He hears a tiny cry. He looks down and sees a kitten. The kitten is all alone. It looks scared. It looks hungry. Tom bends down. He picks up the kitten. He takes it home. Tom feeds the kitten. He asks his parents if he can keep the kitten. They say yes.

What kind of person is Tom?

How do you know?

Skill:

Understanding characters in a story

Answers on page 127.

Where Does a Story Happen?

The place where a story happens is called the **setting.** The setting in a story may be a house, the beach, a school, or a park. The setting helps you understand what happens.

Read the short story. Circle the words that tell you the setting. Draw a line under words that tell you more about the setting. Then answer the questions.

Jan likes to sit in front of her house. She likes to watch what happens on her street. She sees all the different houses. Some houses are painted blue. Others are brown. Jan sees a bus come down the street. It stops at the bus stop. People get on and off the bus. Then the bus roars away. Jan watches the children play. She sees people with shopping bags. She sees people coming home from work. Jan likes her street. There is always something to watch.

What is the setting of this story?

Does Jan live on a farm or in the city?

How do you know?

Skill:

Understanding setting in a story

Answers on page 127.

Why Did It Happen?

Sometimes one thing in a story makes another thing happen. One thing **causes** another thing.

> Stu knew it was going to rain. He got wet <u>because</u> he did not take an umbrella.
>
> Why did Stu get wet? Because he did not take an umbrella.

Read the short story. Then write the cause to answer the questions below.

I really should not eat snacks. If I eat snacks, I can't eat dinner. But today I had some snacks. I ate pizza. I ate hot dogs. I ate cookies and drank soda. Then I went home. It was time for dinner. I looked at the food. I could not eat it because I was too full.

The boy couldn't eat because

The boy shouldn't eat snacks because

Skill:

Recognizing cause and effect

Answers on page 127.

Make a Story

Look at the pictures. Read the sentences. The pictures and sentences tell a story. Write a number in each box to show the correct order of the story.

The bird lays eggs. She sits on the eggs.

A bird builds its nest.

Dan puts up a birdhouse.

The bird feeds her chicks.

The chicks are old enough to fly.

Dan watches the bird-house. He sees a bird visit the birdhouse.

Skill:

Sequencing story events

Answers on page 128.

Tall Tales

Some stories have parts that are true. Other parts are pretend.

> It rained today. So I flew away. I flew above the rain. I did not get wet.
> | | | | |
> true pretend pretend pretend

Read the story. Then read the sentences that follow. Color the fish red if the sentence is true. Color the fish blue if the sentence is pretend.

Mark and Dan went fishing. They took their fishing rods. They brought lunch to eat. They went to the lake. Dan fished in an open spot. Mark fished in a hidden, quiet spot. Later, the boys met for lunch. Mark said, "I got this huge fish." "Where is it?" asked Dan. "It flew away," said Mark. "How big was it?" asked Dan. "It was as big as a car," Mark said. "It was a whale." "There are no whales in the lake," Dan said. "Maybe this whale got lost," Mark said. "It was as big as a tree." The boys looked all along the lake for the whale. They could not find it. "You should have brought it home," Dan said. "Then people would believe you." "I felt sorry for it," Mark said, "so I let it go."

Mark and Dan went fishing.

Mark caught a fish that could fly.

Dan and Mark had lunch together.

Dan and Mark brought their fishing rods to the lake.

Mark caught a fish that was as big as a tree.

Dan did not see the fish that Mark caught.

Skill:

Recognizing fiction

Answers on page 128.

That's the Truth!

Look at the picture. Read each sentence. Circle **true** if the sentence tells something true about the picture. Circle **not true** if the sentence tells something that is not true about the picture.

1. It is a sunny day.	true	not true
2. The boy is carrying an umbrella.	true	not true
3. It is raining hard.	true	not true
4. The boy's feet are wet.	true	not true
5. The girl's head is wet.	true	not true
6. The children are sad.	true	not true

Skill:

Recognizing what is true or not true

Answers on page 128.

What Will Happen?

Some stories tell you what happens. Some stories only give you a hint about what will happen next. They do not tell you what happens. They let you guess what happens. Read the story.

Lynn was drawing. She needed a green crayon. It was on the other side of the table. Lynn reached across the table to get the crayon. She forgot about the glass of water. Her arm hit the glass. "Oh, no," Lynn said.

Draw a picture of what happened next.

Write a sentence telling what happened next.

Skill:

Predicting outcomes

What Do You Think?

Some stories give you hints about what might happen. They may give you hints about what a character might do next. Read the story. Use details from the story to answer the questions below.

Max was a new boy at school. He did not have any friends. In the school yard, Max stood by himself. He watched the other children play. One day, Max saw another boy. The boy smiled at him. Max smiled back. Max thought, "Maybe he will be my friend." Max walked over to the boy. They began to talk.

Is Max a friendly boy?

Will Max and the boy be friends?

Write a sentence about what happens next.

Skill:

Making inferences

108

Answers on page 128.

Read a List

Sometimes you have to read a list. Some lists are in a special order. Have you ever gone out to eat? If you have, you may have ordered food from a list. A list of food is called a **menu.** A menu lists foods in groups. There is a list of salads. There is a list of meat. There is a list of fish. There is a list of sweets.

What's for lunch? Read the menu. The food is listed in groups. What do you want to eat? Circle one food from each group.

Menu

To Start
bread sticks
cheese sticks
salad

Meat and Fish
hamburger
meatballs
fish sticks
tuna salad
hot dog

Sweets
doughnut
cookie
cake
ice cream

Pasta and Pizza
macaroni and cheese
spaghetti
cheese pizza
sausage pizza

Drinks
tomato juice
orange juice
soda
tea or coffee

Side Dishes
peas
string beans
spinach

Skill:

Reading a list

Answers will vary.

Make a List

A list helps you put things in order. A list helps you remember things. Look at the picture of the room. There are many things in the room. Make a list of 10 things in the room. Write each thing next to a number.

1. _____

2. _____

3. _____

4. _____

5. _____

6. _____

7. _____

8. _____

9. _____

10. _____

Skill:

Making a list

Answers on page 128.

Write About You

You are special. You have your own looks. You have your own thoughts. You have your own life. Write about yourself. Write anything you like. Use the lines below to write something about YOU. Write sentences. Remember that the first word in a sentence begins with a capital letter. Remember that a sentence has a subject and a verb. Remember to put a period at the end of each sentence.

Read what you wrote about yourself out loud to another person.

Skill:

Writing sentences

Answers will vary.

Find Word Meanings

You find word meanings in a **dictionary.**

A dictionary is a book that has a list of many words. The words are in the order of the alphabet. The dictionary tells you what each word means. Some dictionaries have pictures to help you.

A sample dictionary is below. Read each word. Read its meanings. Look at the picture. Then answer the questions at the end.

A

actor: a person who acts in a play; someone who plays a role on the stage or in the movies

ant: a small insect that has six legs; ants often live together in large groups

apple: a fruit that grows on a tree; an apple has a core with small seeds inside; apples may be red, green, or yellow

B

bag: something you use to carry things; a bag may have handles; it may be made out of paper, cloth, or plastic

bench: something people sit on; often, a long, wooden seat that many people can sit on; a bench may have a back

bread: a baked food made from flour, water, and other things

C

cap: a small head covering; something people wear on their head

clock: a machine people use to tell the time

cup: something people drink from; also, a measure, as in 1 cup of milk or 1 cup of flour

D

desk: a piece of furniture people use for writing or studying

dish: a plate that people put food on

doll: a toy children play with; a doll is made to look like a person

Answer the questions.

1. How many legs does an ant have?

2. What might a bag be made out of?

3. What are two meanings for the word cup?

Skill:

Using a picture dictionary

Answers on page 128.

Write a Letter

Use the lines below to write a letter to someone.

Remember: A sentence tells a complete thought. A sentence has a subject and a verb. The first word of sentence begins with a capital letter. A sentence ends with a period.

Dear _____,

_____

_____

_____

_____

_____

_____

_____

_____

Sincerely,

_____

Skill:

Writing a letter

Answers will vary.

Address an Envelope

You mail a letter in an envelope. You must write the correct address on an envelope.

Look at the envelope below. It shows what you must write on an envelope. It shows where you write each thing.

return address →

R. Jones
3 Main St.
Anytown, USA Zipcode

stamp →

person's address →

Mrs. Bee Buzzey
24 Hive Road
Bugville, AX 00012

Look at the blank envelope below. Address it to anyone you want. You may make up a pretend address. Write your own name and address in the spot for the return address. Decorate the stamp with a picture.

Skill:

Addressing an envelope

Answers will vary.

Days of the Week

A week has seven days. Each day has a name. A calendar tells the days of the week. Write the days of the week below.

Sunday
_____

Monday
_____

Tuesday
_____

Wednesday
_____

Thursday
_____

Friday
_____

Saturday
_____

On weekdays, people go to school or to work. Weekdays are Monday, Tuesday, Wednesday, Thursday, and Friday. On weekends, most people stay home. They do not go to work or school. Weekend days are Saturday and Sunday.

Skill:

Recognizing the days of the week

Look at the calendar below. Write an S in the boxes of the days you go to school. Write an H in the boxes of the days you do not have to go to school. Say the name of each day as you write.

Sunday	Monday	Tuesday	Wednesday	Thursday	Friday	Saturday

Answers on page 128.

Use a Web

Sometimes a drawing helps you understand a story. You can use a web to help you understand a character in a story. Read the story. Then fill in the web to tell what the main character is like.

My name is Joy. My dad got a new job. Now we live in a new town. At first, I didn't have any friends. Then I saw the girl who lives next door. I said "Hi." She waved at me. The next day, I talked to the girl. Her name is Meg. I asked Meg to come to my house. We went to my room. We played some games. I made lunch for Meg. We talked and we laughed. I'm so happy that I said hello to Meg. Now we are good friends.

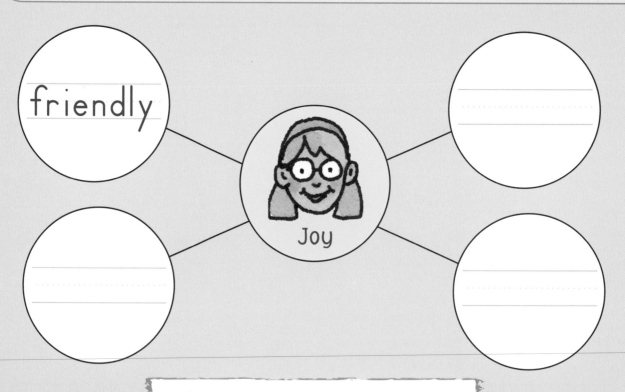

friendly

Joy

Skill:

Using a graphic organizer to aid understanding

118

Answers on page 128.

Use a Chart

Sometimes a chart helps you understand a story. You can use a chart to put things in order. Then you can see the order in which things happen. Read the story.

Sue wanted to have a great party. There were many things she had to do. Sue went to the store. She bought drinks and snacks. When she got home, Sue and her mom baked cookies. Then they blew up balloons. They put the balloons around the room. Sue put out cups, plates, and spoons for her friends. Then she went to her room. She put on a pretty dress. She was ready for the party.

Fill in the chart. Fill in as many boxes as you can. Write what happened in order. One of the boxes is done for you.

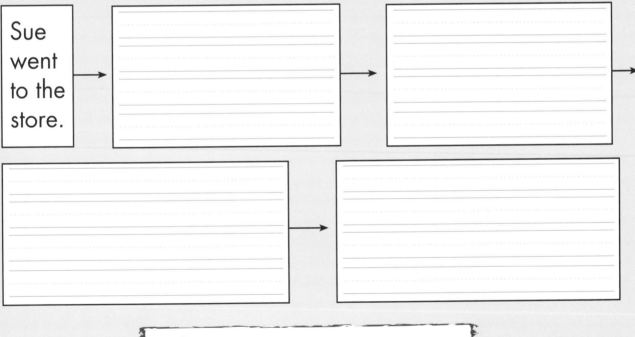

Sue went to the store.

Answers on page 128.

Write and Draw

Now it's time for you to write your own story. You can draw a picture to go with your story. Think about what you will write. You can write about anything. Write on the lines on this page. Draw a picture to go with your story.

Skill:

Writing a story

Answers will vary.

Answer Pages

page 7

page 8

page 9

page 11

page 12

page 13

page 14

page 15

page 16

Listen to the End!

Can you hear it?
Two of the words in each group end with the same sound.
One word ends with a different sound.

Write the word with a different ending on the line below each group of words. Read those words to get the message!
(Hint: Use an uppercase letter for the first word.)

put	ten
dad	your
red	men
Put	**your**
toys	me
cup	see
lip	away
toys	**away**

page 17

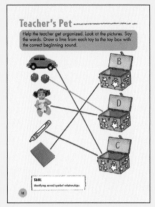

Teacher's Pet

Help the teacher get organized. Look at the pictures. Say the words. Draw a line from each toy to the toy box with the correct beginning sound.

page 18

Sad Dad

Dad can't find his keys! Help him find the right keys. Color in the keys that end in -ad.

page 19

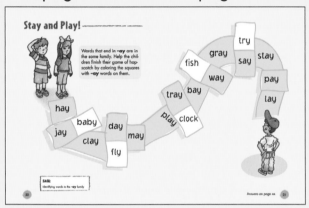

Stay and Play!

Words that end in -ay are in the same family. Help the children finish their game of hopscotch by coloring the squares with -ay words on them.

page 20

page 21

Oh Well

Find the words that end in -ell, and put a circle around them.

The shell they were trying
to sell fell into the well!
Ring the bell! Who can we tell?

page 22

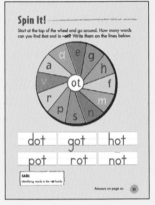

Spin It!

Start at the top of the wheel and go around. How many words can you find that end in -ot? Write them on the lines below.

| dot | got | hot |
| pot | rot | not |

page 23

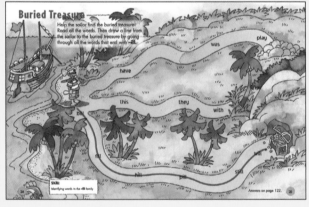

Buried Treasure

Help the sailor find the buried treasure! Read all the words. Then draw a line from the sailor to the buried treasure by going through all the words that end with -ill.

page 24

page 25

Pumpkin Patch

Read the word in each pumpkin. If the word ends with -ake, color the pumpkin orange. Color the other pumpkins green.

cake — there — said
what — take — can
each — bake — your
make — awake — fake

page 26

Be a Word Wizard!

Make new words by changing the beginning sounds of the words below. Use the picture clues to help you. Write the new word on the line. The first one is done for you.

fake	cake
shell	bell
bake	rake
bill	hill
hot	pot
bay	hay

page 27

Color It In!

The letter c has two different sounds. Listen for the hard c sound in cat. Listen for the soft c sound in pencil. Color the hard c words blue. Color the soft c words orange.

What do you see?

page 28

Gone Fishing!

The letter g has two different sounds. Listen for the hard g sound in Gabe. Listen for the soft g sound in Ginger.

Help Gabe catch all the fish that have the hard g sound. Help Ginger catch all the fish that have the soft g sound. Color Gabe's fish blue. Color Ginger's fish red.

page 29

Over the River!

Some vowels make short sounds. Listen for the short vowels in cat, pet, pin, mop, and cup.

Help the scout leader cross the river. Color the short vowels gray. Color the rest of the stones blue. If you color the stones correctly, the scout leader will have a path across the river.

page 31

page 32

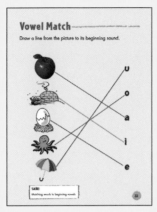

page 33

page 34

page 35

page 36

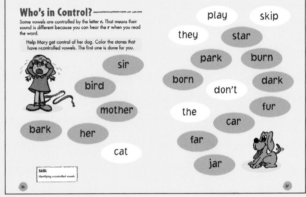

page 37

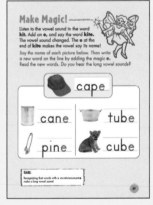

page 38

page 39

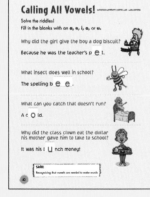

page 40

page 41

page 42

page 43

page 44   page 45   page 46   page 47

page 48   page 49   page 50   page 51

page 52   page 53   page 54   page 55

page 56   page 57   page 58   page 59

page 60

page 61

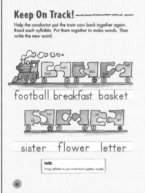

page 62

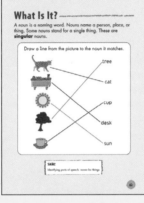

page 63

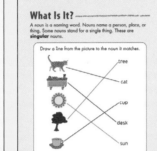

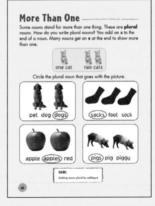

page 64

page 65

page 66

page 67

page 68

page 69

page 70

page 71

page 72

page 73

125

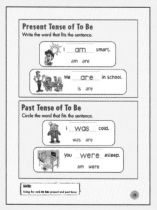

page 75

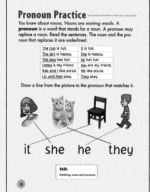

page 76

page 77

page 78

page 79

page 80

page 81

page 82

page 83

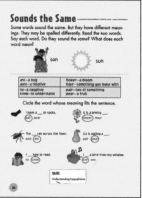

page 84

page 85

page 86

page 87

page 88

page 89

page 90

page 91

page 92

page 93

page 94

page 95

page 98

page 99

page 100

page 101

page 102

page 103

page 104

Make a Story
Look at the pictures. Read the sentences. The pictures and sentences tell a story. Write a number in each box to show the correct order of the story.

4 — The bird lays eggs. She sits on the eggs.
3 — A bird builds its nest.
1 — Dan puts up a birdhouse.
5 — The bird feeds her chicks.
6 — The chicks are old enough to fly.
2 — Dan watches the birdhouse. He sees a bird visit the birdhouse.

Skill: Sequencing story events

page 105

Tall Tales
Some stories have parts that are true. Other parts are pretend.

It rained today. So I flew away. I flew above the rain. I did not get wet.
true   pretend   pretend   pretend

Read the story. Then read the sentences that follow. Color the fish red if the sentence is true. Color the fish blue if the sentence is pretend.

Mark and Dan went fishing. They took their fishing rods. They brought lunch to eat. They went to the lake. Dan fished in an open spot. Mark fished in a hidden, quiet spot. Later, the boys met for lunch. Mark said, "I got this huge fish." "Where is it?" asked Dan. "It flew away," said Mark. "How big was it?" asked Dan. "It was as big as a car," Mark said. "It was a whale." "There are no whales in the lake," Dan said. "Maybe this whale got lost," Mark said. "It was as big as a tree." The boys looked all along the lake for the whale. They could not find it. "You should have brought it home," Dan said. "Then people would believe you." "I tell sorry for it," Mark said, "so I let it go."

- Mark and Dan went fishing.
- Mark caught a fish that could fly.
- Dan and Mark had lunch together.
- Dan and Mark brought their fishing rods to the lake.
- Mark caught a fish that was as big as a tree.
- Dan did not see the fish that Mark caught.

Skill: Recognizing fiction

page 106

That's the Truth!
Look at the picture. Read each sentence. Circle **true** if the sentence tells something true about the picture. Circle **not true** if the sentence tells something that is not true about the picture.

1. It is a sunny day. — not true
2. The boy is carrying an umbrella. — not true
3. It is raining hard. — true
4. The boy's feet are wet. — true
5. The girl's head is wet. — not true
6. The children are sad. — not true

Skill: Recognizing what is true or not true

page 107

What Will Happen?
Some stories tell you what happens. Some stories only give you a hint about what will happen next. They do not tell you what happens. They let you guess what happens. Read the story.

Lynn was drawing. She needed a green crayon. It was on the other side of the table. Lynn reached across the table to get the crayon. She forgot about the glass of water. Her arm hit the glass. "Oh, no," Lynn said.

Draw a picture of what happened next.

Drawings will vary.

Write a sentence telling what happened next. **Sample Answer**

Lynn knocked her glass of water off the table.

Skill: Predicting outcomes

page 108

What Do You Think?
Some stories give you hints about what might happen. They may give you hints about what a character might do next. Read the story. Use details from the story to answer the questions below.

Max was a new boy at school. He did not have any friends. In the school yard, Max stood by himself. He watched the other children play. One day, Max saw another boy. The boy smiled back. Max thought, "Maybe he will be my friend." Max walked over to the boy. They began to talk.

Sample Answers
Is Max a friendly boy? **Yes**
Will Max and the boy be friends? **Yes**
Write a sentence about what happens next.
Max and the boy will become good friends.

Skill: Making inferences

page 110

Make a List
A list helps you put things in order. A list helps you remember things. Look at the picture of the room. There are many things in the room. Make a list of 10 things in the room. Write each thing next to a number. **Sample Answers**

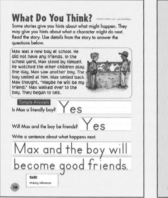

1. bed
2. desk
3. shoes
4. lamp
5. mirror
6. clock
7. poster
8. bear
9. ball
10. pen

Skill: Making a list

page 113

C
cap: a small head covering; something people wear on their head
clock: a machine people use to tell the time
cup: something people drink from; also, a measure, as in 1 cup of milk or 1 cup of flour

D
desk: a piece of furniture people use for writing or studying
dish: a plate that people put food on
doll: a toy children play with; a doll is made to look like a person

Answer the questions.
1. How many legs does an ant have?
SIX
2. What might a bag be made out of?
paper, cloth, or plastic
3. What are two meanings for the word cup?
A cup is something people drink from. A cup is also a measure.

Skill: Using a picture dictionary

page 116

Days of the Week
A week has seven days. Each day has a name. A calendar tells the days of the week. Write the days of the week below.

Sunday — Sunday
Monday — Monday
Tuesday — Tuesday
Wednesday — Wednesday
Thursday — Thursday
Friday — Friday
Saturday — Saturday

On weekdays, people go to school or to work. Weekdays are Monday, Tuesday, Wednesday, Thursday, and Friday. On weekends, most people stay home. They do not go to work or school. Weekend days are Saturday and Sunday.

Skill: Recognizing the days of the week

page 117

Look at the calendar below. Write an S in the boxes of the days you go to school. Write an H in the boxes of the days you do not have to go to school. Say the name of each day as you write.

Sunday	Monday	Tuesday	Wednesday	Thursday	Friday	Saturday
H	S	S	S	S	S	H
H	S	S	S	S	S	H
H	S	S	S	S	S	H
H	S	S	S	S	S	H
H	S	S	S	S	S	H

page 118

Use a Web
Sometimes a drawing helps you understand a story. You can use a web to help you understand a character in a story. Read the story. Then fill in the web to tell what the main character is like.

My name is Joy. My dad got a new job. Now we live in a new town. At first, I didn't have any friends. Then I saw the girl who lives next door. I said "Hi." She waved at me. The next day, I talked to the girl. Her name is Meg. I asked Meg to come to my house. We went to my room. We played some games. I made lunch for Meg. We talked and we laughed. I'm so happy that I said hello to Meg. Now we are good friends.

Sample Answers
Joy — friendly, fun, playful, happy

Skill: Using a graphic organizer to aid understanding

page 119

Use a Chart
Sometimes a chart helps you understand a story. You can use a chart to put things in order. Then you can see the order in which things happen. Read the story.

Sue wanted to have a great party. There were many things she had to do. Sue went to the store. She bought drinks and snacks. When she got home, Sue and her mom baked cookies. Then they blew up balloons. They put the balloons around the room. Sue put out cups, plates, and spoons for her friends. Then she went to her room. She put on a pretty dress. She was ready for the party.

Fill in the chart. Fill in as many boxes as you can. Write what happened in order. One of the boxes is done for you.

| Sue went to the store. | → Sue and her mom baked cookies. | → Then they blew up balloons. |

| Sue put out cups, plates, and spoons. | → Sue put on a pretty party dress. |

Skill: Using a chart to aid understanding of sequence